Estimating Riparian Area Extent and Land Use
in the Midwest

Many different types of riparian areas can be found throughout the seven-State Midwest Region.

Introduction

The ecological and social importance of riparian areas as landscape elements is undisputed (e.g., see Verry *et al.* 2000); however, there is great uncertainty about the cumulative importance of riparian areas in many landscapes and regions. This is a consequence of inadequate inventory data on the extent, type, and land use/land cover of riparian resources. The seven-State Midwest Region of the continental United States is no exception (figure 1). This region is one of the most water-rich areas in the continental United States, yet we are not aware of any general accounting of amount, type, or land use of riparian resources here.

Because of the lack of regional data on riparian resources, it is difficult to determine the degree to which different types of riparian areas receive protection, the extent of change in riparian land use/land cover over time, and the social and economic benefits derived from different types of riparian land use. At issue is the availability and adequacy of riparian resource information used to make policy and management decisions in the region.

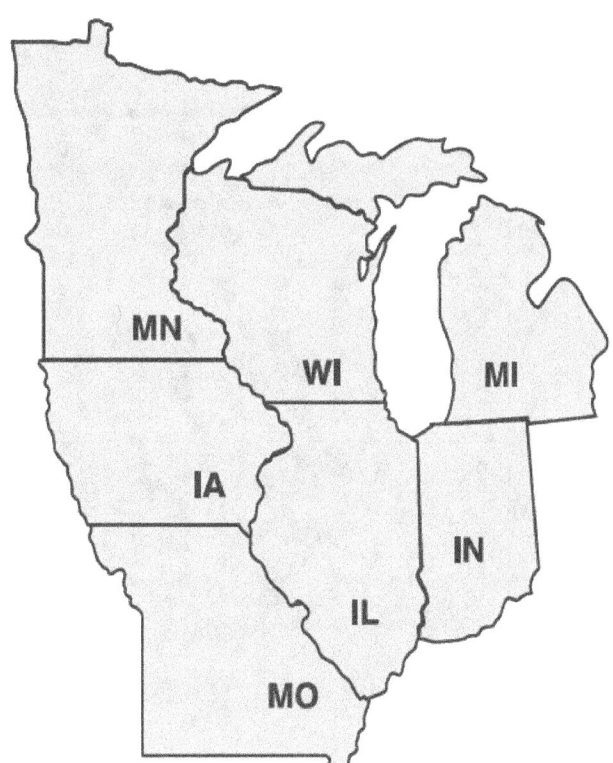

Figure 1.—The seven-State Midwest Region.

A fundamental barrier to adequate assessment of riparian resources is uncertainty over appropriate definitions. We define a riparian area as an ecotone of functional interaction between land and surface water. More specifically, it is that land area that directly influences surface waters and, in turn, is directly influenced by them (figure 2; Ilhardt *et al.* 2000). Under this definition, riparian areas include lands associated with all types of surface waters including lakes, open-water wetlands, rivers, and streams (six different photographic examples of riparian areas are included throughout this report). In other words, riparian areas are not exclusively floodplains, or wetlands, or near-bank environments, nor are they associated only with streams and rivers. Unfortunately, many people continue to view riparian areas under a restricted definition (i.e., streamside forest and floodplains), introducing the potential for gross underestimation of riparian area extent in regional landscapes.

Figure 2.—Stylized representation of a riparian area showing the lateral extent of various ecological interactions between land and water.

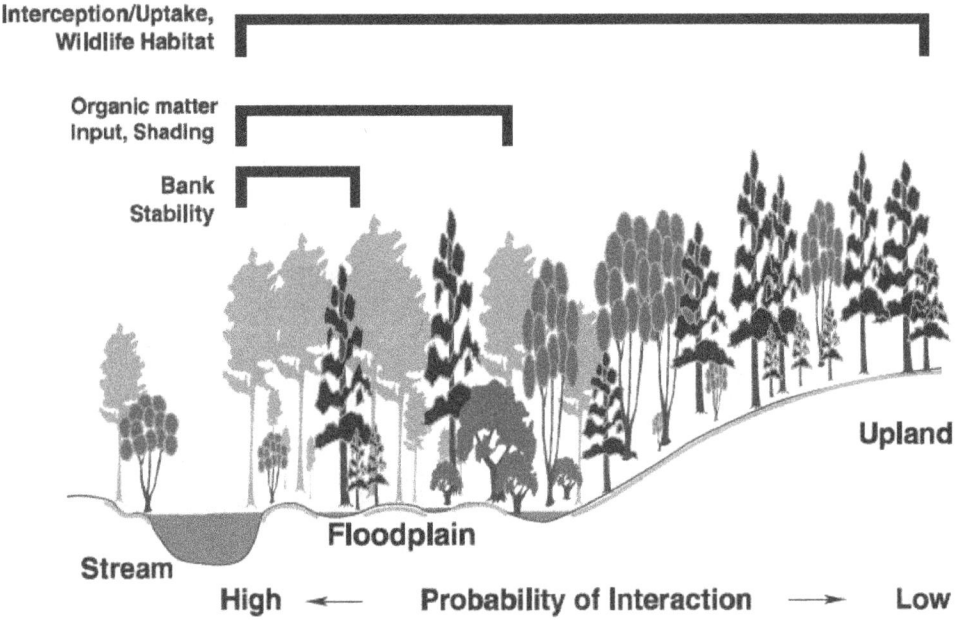

Method of riparian delineation is another factor that influences estimates of riparian resources in a region. Fixed-width approaches for delineation, e.g., 1-pixel buffers (30 m) on Landsat imagery, are common and relatively straightforward to apply (e.g., Hanowski *et al.* 2000). However, fixed-width approaches are tenuous because they have no functional relationship to the actual riparian areas on the ground, which vary naturally in width among and within systems (Palik *et al.* 2000). We believe there is a need to explore the range of variation in riparian extent introduced using different definitions of riparian areas and delineation approaches (e.g., fixed-width approaches, functional approaches, hydric soil-based approaches).

In this report, we quantify the amount of riparian area in the seven-State Midwest Region of the continental United States. Our objective is to assess the physical extent of riparian areas associated with different types of water bodies, i.e., stream, river, lake, and wetland, and to estimate total extent of riparian lands in the region. Additionally, we characterize land use/land cover, e.g., residential, industrial, agriculture, forests, of riparian areas in each State and for the region as a whole. In this assessment, we determine (1) how much of the regional landscape is riparian, (2) how delineation method influences riparian estimates, and (3) how people have altered the characteristics of riparian areas in the region.

Approach

Amount of Riparian Area

We included seven States in the Midwest Region of the continental United States in this analysis (Minnesota, Wisconsin, Iowa, Missouri, Illinois, Indiana, and Michigan). For each State, we assembled 1:100,000 USGS digital line graph (DLG) hydrography data layers on streams, lakes, and wetlands. Hydrography data sets were accessed through each State's geographic data clearinghouse Web site. Each State, however, has modified the DLG after field rectifications. Digital data for streams, lakes, and wetlands were not available for all States. Lake data were not available for Illinois, Iowa, and Indiana. Wetland data were not available for Illinois, Iowa, and Missouri (see section on Caveats and Limitations). Great Lakes shorelines were excluded from our analysis, as were ditches and canals.

We assessed riparian area extent using several different delineation approaches. First, we delineated fixed-width buffers adjacent to all streams, lakes, and wetlands found on the hydrography layers. We delineated both 30-m and 60-m buffers using the BUFFER command within ArcInfo 8.0. From these numbers, we estimated percent of area for each State that is riparian, based on total land area of a State, exclusive of water and wetlands (i.e., upland land area only).

Secondly, we delineated riparian areas using soil characteristics derived from 1:250,000 STASGO data (State Soil Geographic Database; (http://www.ftw.ncrs.usda.gov/stst_data.html). Our intent was to assess riparian extent using criteria that would consider only floodplains, wetlands, and frequently flooded settings, i.e., a restricted definition of a riparian area. For this analysis, we assumed a land area was riparian if it met four criteria:

(1) the soil belonged to hydrologic groups C or D (slow infiltration, impeding or impervious layers, fine texture), or combinations of C or D and other hydrologic groups (A/D, B/D, C/D) (table 1);

(2) the soil was classified as hydric;

(3) the annual flood frequency was frequent (>50 percent probability of an annual flood) or occasional (5-50 percent probability of an annual flood); and

(4) the drainage class was poorly drained (P), very poorly drained (VP), or a combination of poorly drained/somewhat poorly drained (P/SP), or poorly drained/very poorly drained (P/VP) (table 2).

Finally, we estimated riparian extent using a method based on potential for infrequent, but potentially significant interactions between land and water through large magnitude flooding. For this approach, we used the Federal Emergency Management Agency's (FEMA) flood frequency digital data (http://www.fema.gov/mit/tsd/) to determine amount of land area affected by 100-year floods. These data were available in digital format statewide only for Illinois.

Northern hardwoods adjacent to a headwater stream.

Table 1.—Hydrologic classes in the STATSGO database

Hydrology class	Characteristics
A	High infiltration rates. Soils are deep, well drained to excessively drained sands and gravels.
B	Moderate infiltration rates. Deep and moderately deep. Moderately well and well drained soils with moderately coarse textures.
C	Slow infiltration rates. Soils with layers impeding downward movement of water, or soils with moderately fine or fine textures.
D	Very slow infiltration rates. Soils are clayey, have a high water table, or are shallow to an impervious layer.
A/D	Drained/undrained hydrology class of soils that can be drained and are classified.
B/D	Drained/undrained hydrology class of soils that can be drained and are classified.
C/D	Drained/undrained hydrology class of soils that can be drained and classified.

Table 2.—Soil drainage classes in the STATSGO database

Soil drainage class	Characteristics
Excessively drained (E)	Soils have very high and high hydraulic conductivity and low water holding capacity. Depth to water table is more than 6 feet.
Well drained (W)	Soils have intermediate water holding capacity. Depth to water table is more than 6 feet.
Moderately well drained (MW)	Soils have a layer of low hydraulic conductivity, wet state high in the profile. Depth to water table is 3 to 6 feet.
Poorly drained (P)	Soils may have a saturated zone, a layer of low hydraulic conductivity, or seepage. Depth to water table is less than 1 foot.
Somewhat excessively drained (SE)	Soils have a high hydraulic conductivity and low water holding capacity. Depth to water table is more than 6 feet.
Somewhat poorly drained (SP)	Soils commonly have a layer with low hydraulic conductivity, wet state high in profile. Depth to water table is 1 to 3 feet.
Very poorly drained (VP)	Soils are wet to the surface most of the time. Depth to water table is less than 1 foot, or is ponded.

Riparian Land Use

Land use of riparian areas, delineated with 30-m and 60-m buffers, was determined using National Land Cover Data (http://landcover.usgs.gov) for each State. Land cover data are based on 30-m Landsat thematic mapper imagery. There are 19 land cover classes in this classification. We grouped these classes into four broad categories including developed (urban), agricultural, natural/semi-natural, and other (transitional) (table 3). Land cover data were intersected with riparian areas using LATTICECLIP within ArcGrid (ESRI 1999). The percentage of each land cover class found within delineated riparian areas was summarized for the region and by State and hydrologic type (lake, stream, wetland).

Table 3.—Land cover class from the National Land Cover database used in this analysis

A. Developed

1. Low Intensity Residential
2. High Intensity Residential
3. Commercial/Industrial/Transportation
4. Quarries/Strip Mines/Gravel Pits
5. Urban/Recreational Grasses

B. Natural/Semi-natural

6. Deciduous Forest
7. Evergreen Forest
8. Mixed Forest
9. Grasslands/Herbaceous
10. Shrubland
11. Bare Rock/Sand/Clay
12. Woody Wetlands
13. Emergent Herbaceous Wetlands

C. Agriculture

14. Orchards/Vineyards/Other
15. Pasture/Hay
16. Row Crops
17. Small Grains
18. Fallow

D. Other

19. Transitional

Caveats and Limitations

A number of caveat and limitations associated with our data and procedures may influence estimates, restrict accuracy, and argue for caution in interpretation of the results. First, complete hydrologic data were not available for each State. Specifically, we lacked digital lake data for Illinois, Iowa, and Indiana and wetland data for Illinois, Iowa, and Missouri. These omissions resulted in an underestimate of riparian resources for these States. Fortunately, wetlands and lakes are of relatively lesser geographic importance in these States, compared to the northern Lake States of Michigan, Wisconsin, and Minnesota (figure 3). As such, omission of lake and wetland data for these States may not grossly underestimate total extent of riparian area in the region. Second, there is inconsistency in the extent to which intermittent streams are accounted for in each State. Michigan, Wisconsin, and Minnesota stream layers include intermittent streams, either separately or included with perennial streams. We were unable to determine whether intermittent streams are included in the stream hydrography layer for Illinois, Missouri, Iowa, and Indiana. As such, it is possible that riparian areas for the latter States are underestimated. Moreover, intermittent streams are notoriously underrepresented on USGS quad maps because of the difficulty in interpreting these

systems on air photography, particularly in forest settings. As such, stream hydrolayers for all States, even those that specifically identify intermittent channels, likely grossly underestimate these systems. All of the above caveats likely result in an underestimate of total riparian resources in each State and the region as a whole. On the other hand, overlap in riparian buffers among stream, river, and wetland riparian coverages can potentially inflate estimates of riparian area in some States. We did not determine how much overlap occurred, but it likely is only an issue in States where both streams and large wetlands are extensive, including Minnesota, Michigan, and Wisconsin. Finally, our wetland data layers were not restricted to open-water wetlands, as in some assessments (Minnesota Department of Natural Resources 2001). We also included marshes, swamps, and bogs. As such, our estimates of riparian area around wetlands will be higher than estimates that are restricted to open-water wetlands.

Shown above is a black ash forest along a small stream.

Figure 3.—Area of surface water (blue bars) and wetlands (red bars), in thousands of hectares, for each State in the Midwest Region. Source: 1997 U.S. Department of Agriculture Natural Resource Conservation Service, National Forest Inventory (www.nrcs.usda.gov). Wetland area includes only wetlands and deepwater habitats on non-Federal land.

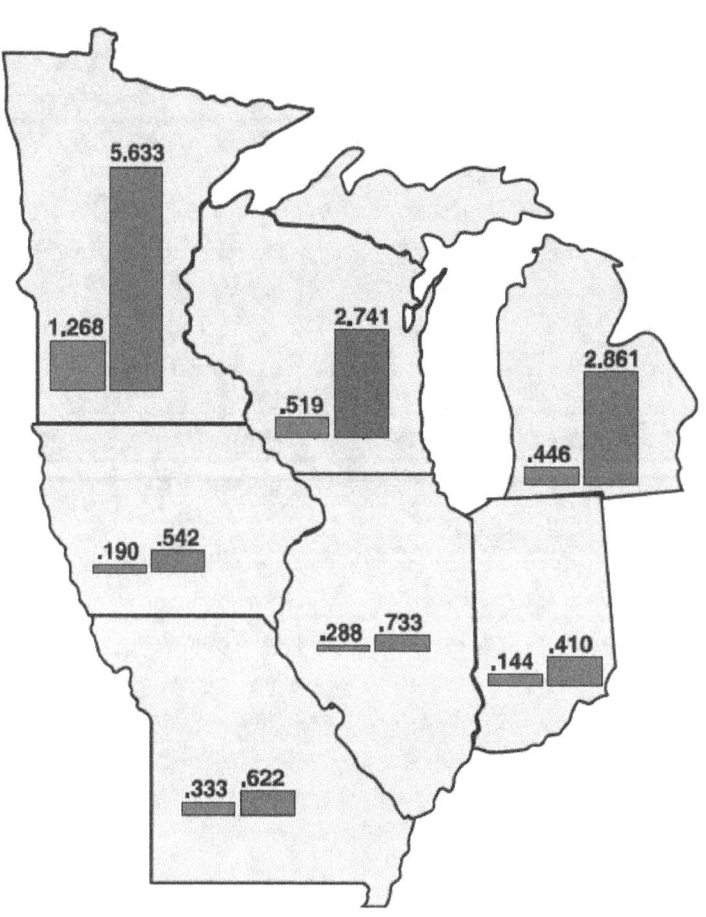

Amount of Riparian Area in the Midwest Region

A Fixed-Width Buffer Approach

We estimate that riparian areas cover at least 8.9 million hectares (based on 30-m buffers) to 13.2 million hectares (60-m buffer) in the seven States, or approximately 8.5 to 12.6 percent of total land area in the region (figure 4). The estimate does not double from 30-m to 60-m buffers because of increased overlap between adjacent water bodies as buffer width increases.

Amount of riparian area varies widely among States, ranging from 4.7 million hectares in Minnesota to 0.3 million hectares in Iowa (based on a 60-m buffer; figure 5). Approximately 77 percent of the regional total occurs in Minnesota, Wisconsin, and Michigan (figure 6). We estimate that up to 17 to 23 percent (based on a 60-m buffer) of the land base in these States is riparian, compared to 2 to 20 percent in Missouri, Iowa, Indiana, and Illinois (figure 7). Estimates of riparian land areas for some States (MN, WI, MI, IN) do not double between 30-m and 60-m buffers; these States included wetland data layers. States that lacked wetland data (IL, MO, IA) had approximately double the land area in 60-m riparian buffers as in 30-m buffers. This indicates that overlap among adjacent wetlands, as buffer width increases, largely drives the nonlinear relationship between buffer width and riparian land area at the regional scale.

Our assessment of riparian extent in the region must be interpreted with caution, because we rely on data and procedural assumptions that decrease accuracy or alter estimates, relative to other assessments. Two assumptions likely lead to an underestimate of total riparian resources in some States and in the region, while a third likely overestimates riparian resources in some States.

The lack of digital hydrologic data on wetlands and lakes for some States (see Approach) and the generally poor inventories of intermittent streams in most States result in underestimates of total riparian area in individual States and the region. Conversely, an undetermined amount of overlap among data layers, particularly stream and wetland data layers in States where both of these resources are abundant, may inflate the total extent of

…our estimates of amount of riparian area for individual States may differ from other assessments due to differences in scale of data layers, definitions of land area, and types of water bodies and wetlands included in the survey.

riparian area for these States and the region. Finally, our estimates of amount of riparian area for individual States may differ from other assessments due to differences in scale of data layers, definitions of land area, and types of water bodies and wetlands included in the survey. For example, using a 60-m buffer, others have estimated the total amount of riparian area in Minnesota at 3.1 million hectares (Minnesota Department of Natural Resources 2001), 34 percent below our estimate of 4.7 million hectares for the State. The difference is likely due to wetland types in our definition, not just open-water wetlands, as in the other survey.

Figure 4.—Cumulative land area and cumulative riparian area, based on 30-m and 60-m buffers, respectively, for the Midwest Region.

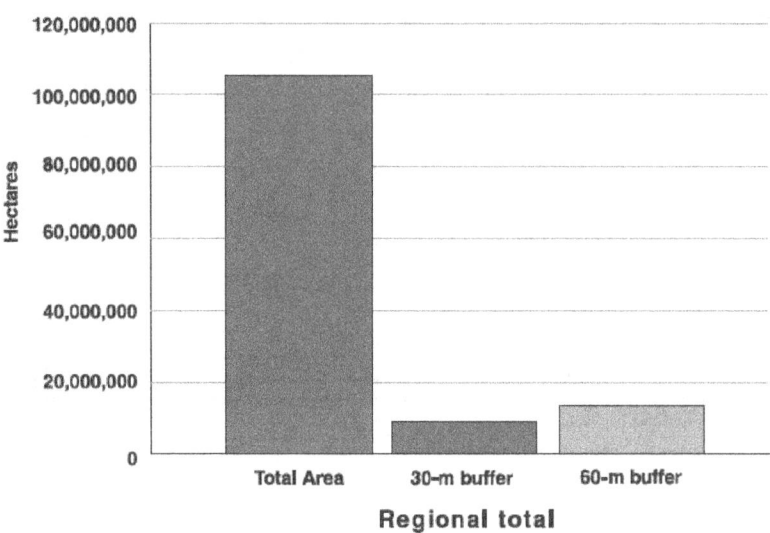

Figure 5.—Total land area (blue bars) and riparian land area, based on 30-m (red bars) and 60-m (yellow bars) buffers, for each State in the Midwest Region. Values are thousands of hectares.

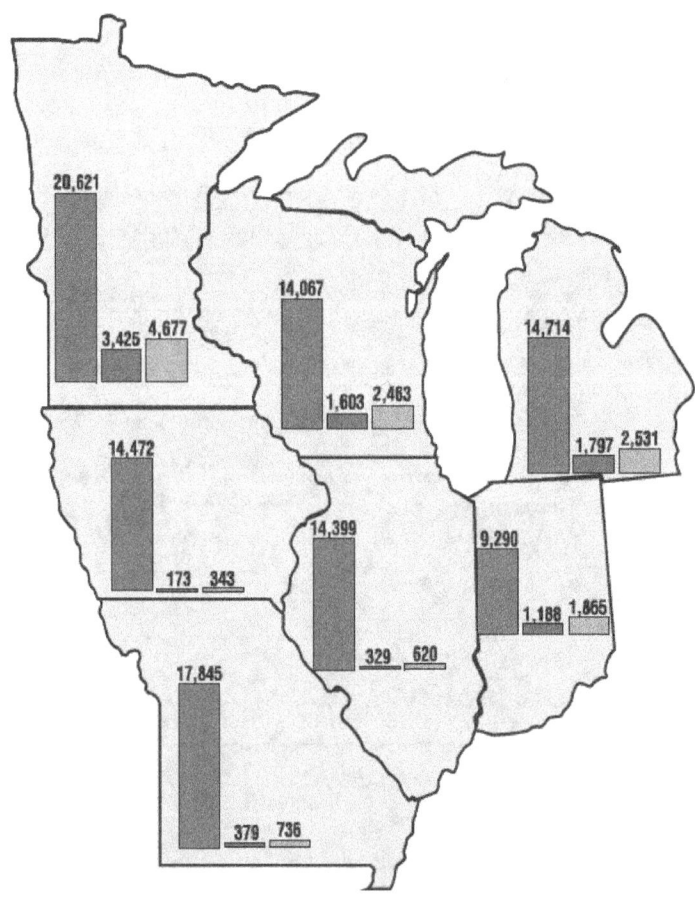

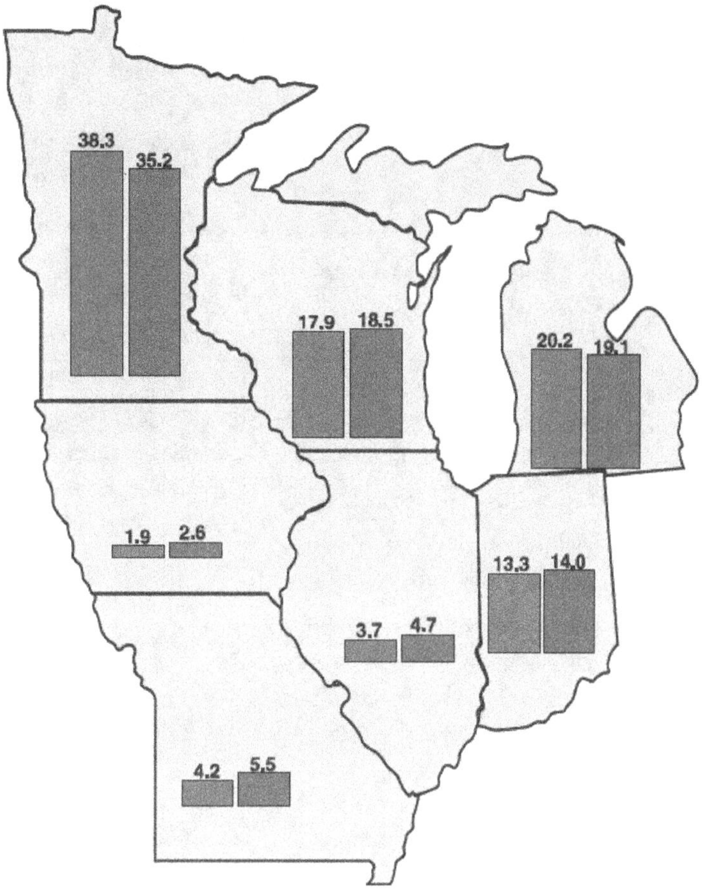

Figure 6.—Percent
contribution by State to
total riparian area in the
Midwest Region based
on 30-m (blue bars)
and 60-m (red bars)
buffers, respectively.

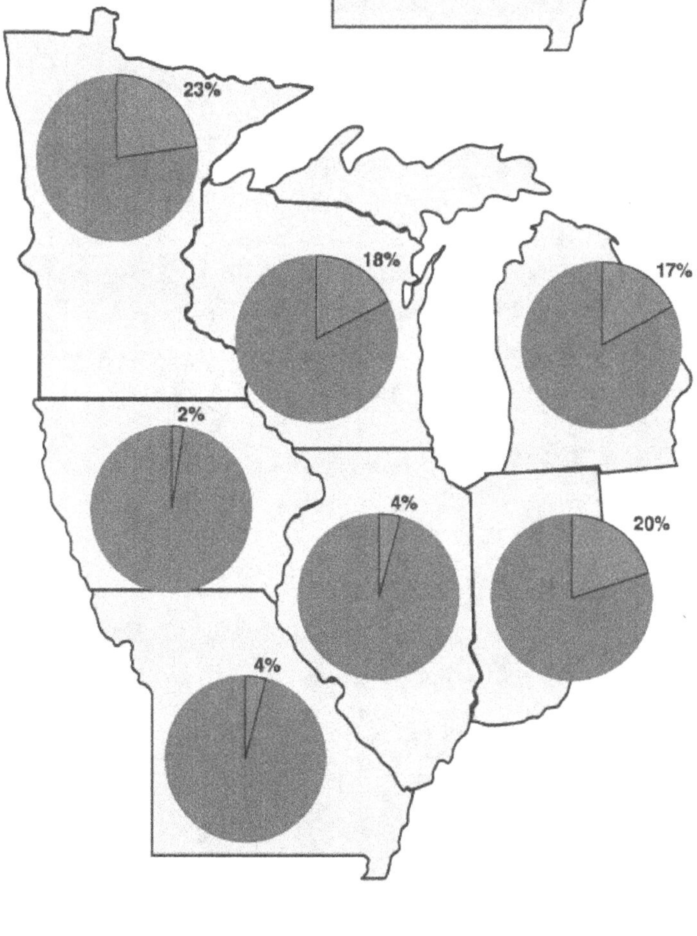

Figure 7.—Percent riparian
area by State in the
Midwest Region. Blue
slices represent percent
of total land area that is
riparian in a State, based
on 60-m buffer around all
water bodies.

Alternative Delineation: Hydric Soil and Flood Probability Indicators

We sought to contrast estimates of riparian area extent based on fixed-width buffers with alternative approaches to delineation, including one that was more restrictive (i.e., equating riparian areas with wetlands and floodplains) and one that was functionally based (e.g., land area influenced by infrequent, ecosystem-altering floods). The alternative approaches we used included (1) riparian delineation using hydric soil indicators and (2) delineation based on 100-year flood probability data. Both were derived from readily available, although not geographically complete, digital data sources. Estimates based on these approaches are provided simply as points of comparison with the buffer-based approach. We make no claims as to their accuracy in reflecting actual riparian extent.

Assessment of riparian area based on hydric soil characteristics generally differs greatly from results based on the fixed-width buffer analysis (table 4). For three States (MN, WI, IN), the restrictive delineation underestimates the amount of riparian area by an order of magnitude, compared to 30-m or 60-m fixed-width buffers. Conversely, for Iowa, this approach increases the riparian estimate by an order of magnitude (table 4), perhaps because the buffer analysis omitted wetland data for this State, while the soil-based approach included wetlands by definition. For Missouri, riparian area estimates based on hydric soil conditions and the 60-m buffer were nearly identical, while the soil estimate for Illinois fell midway between the 30-m and 60-m buffer estimates (table 4).

Probability data for 100-year floods were available statewide in digital format only for Illinois. Our estimate of riparian area using this approach reflects a longer term perspective to land-water interactions. This longer term perspective is not without precedent. Research in other regions has demonstrated that infrequent, large magnitude floods can have important ecosystem-altering effects outside of a floodplain, including extensive vegetation mortality (Michener *et al.* 1998, Palik 1999). Using these data, we estimated Illinois riparian area at nearly 1.6 million hectares, substantially higher than either soil or buffer estimates (table 4).

Open-water wetland in an urbanized area.

Table 4.—Riparian area (hectares) based on soil characteristics, fixed-width buffers, and flood indicators

State	Soil	30-m buffer	60-m buffer	FEMA flood rating[2]
Minnesota	429,807	3,424,776	4,677,041	
Iowa	1,193,446	173,154	342,825	
Illinois	497,655	329,082	619,940	1,583,303
Wisconsin	265,374	1,602,854	2,462,914	
Indiana	314,009	1,188,386	1,864,936	
Missouri	729,121	378,821	736,338	
Michigan	[1]	1,796,911	2,531,346	

[1]Soil data incomplete for Michigan.

[2]Available only for Illinois.

Types of Riparian Areas in the Midwest Region

Regionally, about 48 percent of total riparian lands (based on the mean of 30-m and 60-m buffers) are associated with wetlands, while 36 percent are associated with streams and rivers and 16 percent with lakes (table 5). But the results must be interpreted with caution, because several States (IL, IA, IN, MO) did not have lake or wetland hydrology data available. Consequently, stream riparian areas in these States are overrepresented as a percent of total riparian area. On the other hand, wetlands and lakes in these States are much less extensive than in the northern Lake States (MI, WI, MN; figure 3). Consequently, the lack of accounting for wetlands or lakes in some States may not overly bias our regional results. Moreover, a full accounting of wetlands in all States would only serve to emphasize that most riparian areas in the region are associated wetlands, rather than streams and rivers.

Table 5.—Riparian area (hectares) by type in the seven midwestern States based on 30-m and 60-m buffers

State	30-m buffer			60-m buffer		
	Stream	Wetland	Lake	Stream	Wetland	Lake
Minnesota	601,543	2,646,383	176,850	1,401,850	2,928,551	346,640
Iowa	173,154	na	na	342,825	na	na
Illinois	329,082	na	na	619,940	na	na
Wisconsin	425,979	1	1,176,876	1,062,882	1	1,400,032
Indiana	277,336	911,050	na	557,613	1,307,323	na
Missouri	318,945	na	59,875	641,624	na	94,714
Michigan	494,400	1,232,540	69,971	988,800	1,409,641	132,904
Total	2,620,439	4,789,973	1,483,572	5,615,534	5,646,515	1,974,291
Percent	29.5	53.9	16.7	42.4	42.7	14.9

[1]Lake and wetland data combined for Wisconsin.

Land Use of Riparian Areas in the Midwest Region

Riparian lands in the Midwest support 18 of 19 possible land cover classes (table 6). According to our analysis, fallow lands were nonexistent in riparian areas of the region and thus are not included in the agricultural category. We grouped 17 classes into three broad categories including developed, natural/semi-natural, and agriculture (table 6). The 18th class, transitional land cover, was rare in the region (table 6) and was excluded from further consideration.

Based on our groupings, approximately 72 percent of midwestern riparian areas support natural or semi-natural land cover, including forest, emergent wetland vegetation, natural grassland, or shrubland (figure 8). Within the natural/semi-natural grouping, forest (deciduous, evergreen, mixed, and woody wetland) is the predominant land cover in all States. Another 26 percent of riparian area in the region has been converted to agriculture, while 1.4 percent has been converted to developed (urban/suburban) land uses (figure 8).

There is large variation in riparian land cover among the seven midwestern States (table 6, figure 9). The northern Lake States (MN, WI, MI) contain the greatest amounts of natural/semi-natural riparian areas (73-81 percent, based on 60-m buffers), compared to the Farm Belt States (IA, IN, IL, MO; 38-55 percent). Conversely, the latter States have a much higher percentage of agricultural conversion of riparian areas (43-58 percent), compared to Minnesota, Wisconsin, and Michigan (18-26 percent).

Developed land cover in riparian areas is higher in the Farm Belt States (2-4 percent) than the northern Lake States (1 percent), but still low

overall (table 6, figure 9). Even Illinois, arguably the most urbanized State in the region, has only 3 percent of riparian lands in the developed class (figure 9).

Data interpretation and definitions will affect estimates of riparian land use within individual States. Again, using Minnesota as our example, we found much less agricultural conversion in riparian areas (20 percent, based on a 60-m buffer) than in a similar assessment (50 percent; Minnesota Department of Natural Resources 2001).

…approximately 72 percent of midwestern riparian areas support natural or semi-natural land cover, including forest, emergent wetland vegetation, natural grassland, or shrubland.

Conversely, we found much more woody wetland vegetation (45 percent) in riparian buffers than did the earlier assessment (11 percent). Our inclusion of all wetland types, not just open-water wetlands, likely accounts for these differences. Not only did our estimate include a greater amount of riparian area associated with wetlands, but also swamps, marshes, and bogs are more likely to be associated with wetland forest around their periphery than with agricultural land.

Table 6.—Riparian area (hectares) of the seven midwestern States in different land use/land cover classes
See table 3 for complete land cover descriptors

Land use	State					
	Minnesota		Iowa		Illinois	
	Buffer width		Buffer width		Buffer width	
	30-m	60-m	30-m	60-m	30-m	60-m
Developed						
Low Intensity Residential	4,028	9,681	980	2,037	3,619	7,096
High Intensity Residential	1,261	2,776	169	386	1,150	2,405
Commercial/Industrial/Transportation	7,718	15,151	4,203	7,219	2,807	5,345
Quarries/Strip Mines/Gravel Pits	2,926	4,545	108	213	400	691
Urban/Recreational Grasses	2,299	4,950	310	771	2,992	6,016
Natural/Semi-natural						
Deciduous Forest	315,589	548,262	49,061	86,762	82,253	154,340
Evergreen Forest	103,099	158,642	217	381	6,925	10,863
Mixed Forest	100,839	166,127	529	973	3,876	6,766
Grasslands/Herbaceaous	711	1,191	6,585	13,555	3,577	6,989
Shrubland	23,456	30,885	0	0	51	94
Bare Rock/Sand/Clay	69	172	813	1,028	313	540
Woody Wetlands	1,882,200	2,112,904	22,575	37,536	64,536	104,339
Emergent Herbaceaous Wetlands	559,805	694,038	7,588	12,182	13,084	17,187
Agriculture						
Orchards/Vineyards/Other	0	0	0	0	6	15
Pasture/Hay	154,479	307,327	25,935	54,669	60,109	121,996
Row Crops	238,578	572,474	52,995	122,551	82,879	174,013
Small Grains	17,211	32,996	1,086	2,561	501	1,235
Other						
Transitional	10,507	14,921	0	0	3	10

State								
Wisconsin		Indiana		Missouri		Michigan	
Buffer width		Buffer width		Buffer width		Buffer width	
30-m	60-m	30-m	60-m	30-m	60-m	30-m	60-m
3,192	8,110	17,496	27,972	1,677	3,366	7,174	14,711
1,005	2,521	2,766	4,319	371	737	1,894	3,770
4,006	9,135	10,714	16,309	2,469	4,516	5,352	9,905
282	480	2,064	3,724	255	481	2,221	4,632
2,163	4,947	6,112	10,027	1,415	2,973	2,321	4,632
421,314	690,341	287,723	433,148	112,489	213,134	280,430	458,508
51,088	82,904	17,338	27,851	12,111	21,330	90,017	133,186
101,687	158,848	6,665	8,635	15,008	27,638	65,777	105,260
15,100	22,497	7,101	11,411	5,285	11,101	14,802	22,555
70	85	104	186	277	604	114	178
457	558	239	419	1,180	1,753	213	328
507,233	611,703	123,276	141,142	72,754	117,073	902,276	1,112,234
203,252	233,438	22,946	26,085	11,830	18,177	185,340	219,325
14	14	0	0	0	0	1	1
116,614	272,100	150,743	305,352	58,664	132,810	49,910	92,833
173,052	361,760	350,594	670,783	78,784	171,107	187,006	348,028
25	102	178	347	4,163	9,347	44	93
2,301	3,372	1,700	2,916	89	191	2,019	3,078

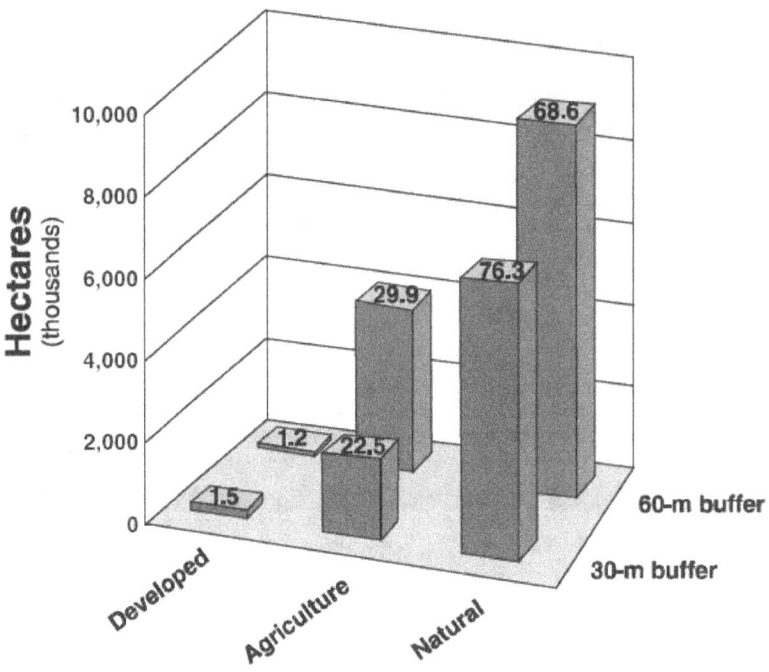

Figure 8.—Riparian land use in the Midwest Region based on 30-m and 60-m buffers. Percentages are portions of total riparian area in the region.

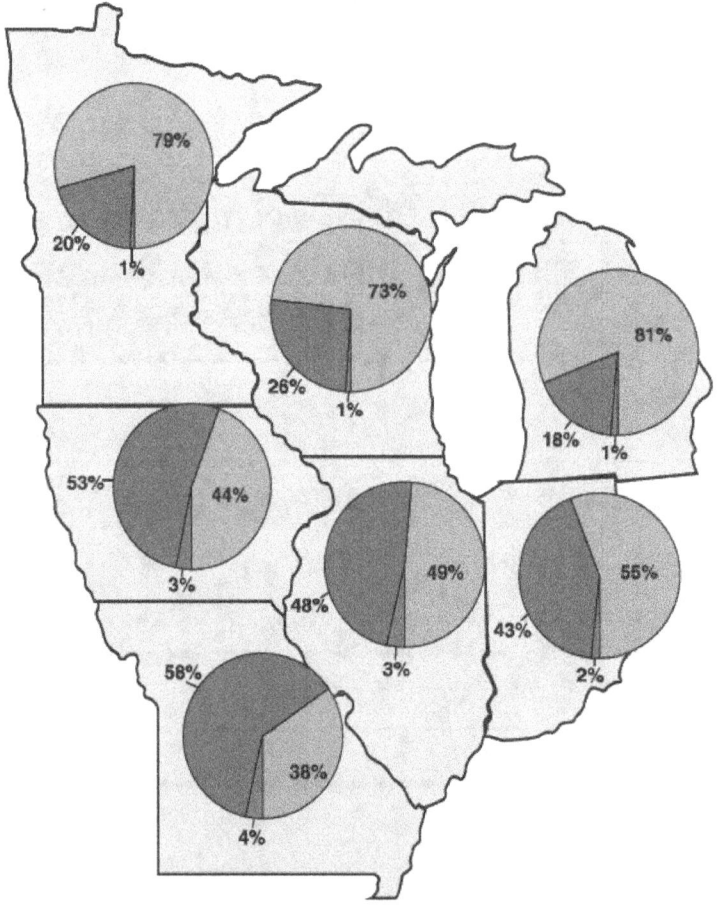

Figure 9.—Riparian land use in the Midwest Region. Colors represent percentages of riparian lands in different land cover categories (red is agriculture, yellow is natural land cover, blue is urban/developed).

Implications and Needs

Amount of Riparian Area

Our estimates of riparian land area for several of the midwestern States, and consequently the region as a whole, are conservative due to data limitations. Nonetheless, the magnitude of the estimates point to substantial ecological, social, and economic importance of riparian resources in the region, particularly for the upper Great Lake States of Minnesota, Wisconsin, and Michigan.

Several potential implications are suggested by these data. For example, policies that result in restricted land use for forestry or agriculture within riparian areas could have significant negative impacts on local and regional economies. For instance, Minnesota contains 6.1 million hectares of productive forest land (Shifley and Sullivan 2002), of which 23 percent, or1.4 million hectares, potentially is riparian. Restrictive or no-harvest policies for 1.4 million hectares of productive riparian forests would have measurable negative economic consequences for the State. Conversely, the cumulative importance of riparian resources in Minnesota and the region as a whole suggests that policies and practices that significantly degrade riparian habitat will have broad negative impacts on wildlife populations, water quality, and biotic diversity. Understanding multidimensional ecological and economic responses to different amounts and types of riparian protection is an important policy need.

Our analysis demonstrates how a riparian delineation approach might influence policy and management decisionmaking. An example of this is the nonlinear relationship between riparian buffer width and amount of riparian land area. For the region as a whole, doubling riparian buffer width from 30 m to 60 m results in only a 49-percent increase in riparian land area. This same nonlinearity is evident for all States that include wetland data layers (MN, WI, MI, IN). One policy interpretation of this is that doubling riparian management buffer widths throughout a State or region, while presumably resulting in greater ecological protection of aquatic ecosystems and water quality, will not double the amount of land area potentially falling into use-restricted riparian management area designations. The shape of the response function between riparian management buffer width and ecological function needs better clarification before the economic and social consequences of riparian area delineation can be fully appreciated.

Types of Riparian Areas

At the regional scale, the majority of midwestern riparian land area is associated with wetlands. This is an important result because most people equate riparian areas strictly with stream ecosystems. Clearly, this is not the case for much of the region. Similarly, lake riparian areas, although not as extensive as those associated with streams or wetlands, are a significant resource in the region. The role that lake and wetland riparian management zones have in protecting ecological functions in associated water bodies is greatly understudied relative to streams.

The generally poor accounting of intermittent channels in hydrologic data layers for the Midwest likely leads to large, but underdetermined, underestimates of the amount of total and stream-associated riparian land area. Spatial data on intermittent streams are notoriously incomplete, because of difficulty in identifying small streams using air photography. With better inventory, it is likely that the amount of stream riparian areas would increase, perhaps even exceeding that associated with wetlands in some States.

A bottomland hardwood forest along a river.

Riparian Land Use

On the surface, the large amount of riparian land area in natural/semi-natural land cover classes suggests that riparian functions, including sediment filtering, carbon storage, and wildlife habitat, are being maintained in the region. Although this is an encouraging result, it must be interpreted with caution. Natural land cover classes impart only limited information about ecosystem structure and function. They say nothing about vegetation age, species composition, or local disturbances that can degrade riparian functionality. Moreover, our assessment of riparian land use/land cover, based on the fixed-width buffer approach, is limited to at the most first 60 m of land around or adjacent to lakes, wetlands, and streams. Protection of water quality and aquatic habitat is equally dependent on land use and cover in the larger watersheds outside of the riparian area. Our assessment does not account for condition in the watershed proper.

The regional extent of land cover conversion in riparian areas to agricultural or other development is likely underestimated because of poor documentation of intermittent streams. For example, in Michigan, 61 percent of riparian areas associated with documented intermittent streams have been converted to agriculture, or are in developed urban areas, compared to 19 percent of riparian areas in the State as a whole. Better inventory and accounting of intermittent streams in the region would likely increase the estimate of riparian land that is in agriculture or otherwise developed. Advanced remote sensing methodologies are needed to better document intermittent and small perennial stream locations and associated land use/land cover.

Sedge meadow along a small stream.

Key Points

1. Cumulatively, riparian areas occupy up to 13 percent of the land base in the seven-State Midwest Region.

2. Riparian area, as a percent of total land area, exceeds 17 percent in four midwestern States (MN, WI, MI, IN).

3. Amount of riparian area is likely underestimated in each State and the region due to limitations of available data, particularly the poor accounting of intermittent streams.

4. For some States, and the region as a whole, doubling the width of a riparian buffer from 30 to 60 m results in only a 49 percent increase in estimated riparian area, due to increasing overlap between adjacent riparian areas as buffer width increases.

5. In the region, 72 percent of riparian areas are in natural/semi-natural land use categories, with forests making up the majority of this total. Agricultural land use in riparian areas is more important in the Farm Belt States (MO, IN, IL, IA), but still less than 60 percent of total riparian area.

6. Urban development in riparian areas is low for the region as a whole, and in each State, totaling no more than 4 percent of any State's total riparian resource.

7. Condition of the watershed outside of the riparian area is not accounted for in our assessment of land use, but has a large influence on water quality and aquatic habitat integrity not reflected in riparian land use and condition.

Literature Cited

Hanowski, J.M.; Wolter, P.T.; Niemi, G.J. 2000. Effects of riparian buffers on landscape characteristics: implications for breeding birds. In: Wignington, P.J., Jr.; Beschta, R.B.L., eds. Riparian ecology and management in multi-land use watersheds. Proceedings of the Journal of American Water Resources Association: 523-528.

Ilhardt, B.L.; Verry, E.S.; Palik, B.J. 2000. Defining riparian areas. In: Verry, E.S.; Hornbeck, J.W.; Dolloff, C.A., eds. Riparian management in forests of the continental eastern United States. Boca Raton, FL: Lewis Publishers: 23-42.

Michener, W.K.; Blood, E.R.; Brim Box, J.M.; Couch, C.A.; Golladay, S.W.; Hippe, D.J.; Kirkman, L.K.; Mitchell, R.J.; Palik, B.J. 1998. Tropical storm flooding of a Coastal Plain landscape. BioScience. 48: 696-705.

Minnesota Department of Natural Resources. 2001. Riparian forests in Minnesota: a report to the state legislature.

Palik, B.J.; Michener, W.K.; Mitchell, R.J.; Edwards, D. 1999. The effects of landform and plant size on mortality and recovery of longleaf pine during a 100-year flood. Ecoscience. 6: 255-263.

Palik, B.J.; Zasada, J.; Hedman, C. 2000. Ecological considerations for riparian silviculture. In: Verry, E.S.; Hornbeck, J.W.; Dolloff, C.A., eds. Riparian management in forests of the continental eastern United States. Boca Raton, FL: Lewis Publishers: 233-254.

Shifley, S.R.; Sullivan, N.H. 2002. The status of timber resources in the north central United States. Gen. Tech. Rep. NC-228. St. Paul, MN: U.S. Department of Agriculture, Forest Service, North Central Research Station. 50 p.

Verry, E.S.; Hornbeck, J.W.; Dolloff, C.A., eds. 2000. Riparian management in forests of the continental eastern United States. Boca Raton, FL: Lewis Publishers. 402 p.

About the Authors

Brian Palik is a Research Ecologist and Project Leader for the USDA Forest Service North Central Research Station, Grand Rapids, MN.

Swee May Tang is a graduate student at the University of Washington, Seattle, WA.

Quinn Chavez is a GIS Specialist with the USDA Forest Service Northeastern Area State and Private Forestry, St. Paul, MN.

Palik, Brian; Tang, Swee May; Chavez, Quinn.
2004. Estimating riparian area extent and land use in the Midwest.
Gen. Tech. Rep. NC-248. St. Paul, MN: U.S. Department of Agriculture, Forest Service, North Central Research Station. 28 p.

This report quantifies the amount and land use/land cover of riparian area in the seven-State Midwest Region of the continental United States. We estimate that riparian areas cover 8.9 to 13.2 million hectares in the region and that approximately 72 percent of riparian areas support natural or semi-natural land cover.

Key Words: Riparian area, Midwest, riparian buffers, land use, land cover

www.ingramcontent.com/pod-product-compliance
Lightning Source LLC
Chambersburg PA
CBHW080758290526
45790CB00008B/3499